MW00904085

# This Sketchbook Belongs to

______________________________